Unraveling
Coming Out and Back Together

The gift of unraveling
is becoming. may we
all embrace this gift

Rebecca

Poems by Rebecca Wilson

WWW.TEHOMCENTER.ORG

Unraveling: Coming Out and Back Together
ISBN: 978-1-960326-70-6

Tehom Center Publishing is a 501c3 non-profit imprint of Parson's Porch Books. Tehom Center Publishing celebrates feminist and queer authors, with a commitment that at least half our authors are people of color. Its face and voice is Rev. Dr. Angela Yarber.

Unraveling

Dedication

To my circle of Wise Women. Your love, light, legacy, and lipstick marks held me together in my season of unraveling.

Honoring

my mother, Jo-Ann Snyder
my dearest friend, Joanne Snedden

Remembering

Clara Webb
Jacqueline Washington
Amanda Gudme
Grace Bazmore
Wendy Hamilton
Barbara Lewis-Lakin
Lois Rutt

Acknowledgements

I have come to understand gratitude as a spiritual practice. So, acknowledging my gratitude to all those who make this collection of poetry a reality is the easiest note to write. Thank you to everyone who has ever read my poems, offered feedback, made grammatical corrections (reminding me how to use there/their/they're), spoken words of affirmation, and encouraged me to share my poetry with a wider audience. Thank you to everyone who has gifted me journals and pens, inspirational room to create, safe space to unravel, and the courage to tell my story.

Contents

Introduction

I purchased my first and only clergy robe at a Catholic book store on a clearance rack. It was simple and that's what excited me most. There were a few loose strings hanging from the bottom hem. I left them there for fear that one pull and it would all unravel.

Everything did unravel.

These poems piece together a story told in a pattern of liturgical seasons, weaving throughout the most painful and liberating season of my life. In February 2017 I surrendered my credentials as a provisional deacon in the United Methodist Church. Months prior, rather than submitting my papers for full ordination to the Board of Ordained Ministry, I sent a letter coming out as lesbian, sharing the decision to leave the ordination process.

The decision to leave the denomination of my birth, baptism, confirmation, and commissioning was not merely so that I could live authentically as a queer lesbian woman, it was about claiming my freedom from a life of shame. My life was shrouded with heavy garments of a childhood marked by emotional and sexual abuse. My first coming out experience was blanketed with responses that my sexuality was not only sinful, but a symptom of mental illness and a result of sexual abuse. I could not continue healing from the abuse while continuing to deny my sexuality. I could not embrace my sexuality and continue serving as clergy in the United Methodist Church. I was in an impossible position, forced to make an impossible choice.

Since that February day, life has felt like both a somber funeral and a festive parade. On another February day in 2019, I was in St. Louis, Missouri, witness to the UMC Special General Conference. As voting results were projected on the screen my heart broke, more sharply than it did two years earlier. This time my brokenness was caught on camera and the rights sold for all to share. That photo captured the grieving, but it does not tell my story. My story is so much more than grief.

It's impossible to tell the story of my life without talking about the United Methodist Church. It's a part of me. It's deep—like tree roots—specifically the roots of the trees my grandfather planted in honor of his granddaughters at the church where five generations of our family belonged. I sometimes wish the roots didn't exist, that I could sever the ties. Then I remember, the connection isn't dependent on church membership or clergy credentials. It hinges on something much stronger than a robe or a stole.

The Sunday I came out to my home church in an Advent sermon on fear, a beloved saint called me over. Tearfully shaking her first in the air. "Oh, this church…" she cried. As she leaned in to hug me, her lips grazed the collar of my robe. I later prayerfully and intentionally unraveled that robe thread by thread. I kept one small square with her lipstick still visible on the frayed edges. There are days and seasons I tuck it into my pocket as a reminder of her love for me and God's love for us all.

These poems tell a story that I once thought I needed permission to share. I learned while waiting that people in power fear the power of stories. The power of one story is the way it inspires another. I'm changed by the stories of others and I hope in some way my story impacts you.

This story is not limited to a particular denomination or faith. It's about the slow death that comes from believing your life has no value, and the new life that begins when you courageously embrace who you are and where you've been. This is a story of the life that comes when we unravel the shame that keeps us from living.

Everything did unravel. Only then could it come together.

{Ordinary}

Pulse

when I was little I could never find my pulse by putting my fingers on
my wrist
but I could feel it in that little indent at the place where your throat
meets your neck
well, that's how I described it

I remember my swimming teacher telling me I couldn't
that's not possible
I remember pleading with her
I'm not kidding, I feel it, right here
putting my fingers in that little indent where my throat met my neck

tonight, I'm sitting on the back deck looking up to the sky
even though it's raining heavy, I had to come outside to breathe
to feel my pulse
even though my blood is pumping, hard and fast
and has been that way for days
there've been moments when I've wondered
am I still alive
is that my heart beating or is that pulse the sound of my heart being
beaten
either way, my heart is broken
I'm broken, shattered, scattered into pieces
like those bodies in Pulse's bathroom and on the dance floor
like the bouncer who was no match for a crazed gunman at the door
like mothers texting, calling, pleading for a response
for their phone to ring, or vibrate, or pulse
anything better than silence

my heart is bleeding, like it was the day before
when I opened a long-hidden vein and let the truth drain out
there was no perfect way to say it
I'd been practicing it for months, for years really, a lifetime
every morning and evening checking for a pulse
not with fingers pressed into my wrist
but into that little indent where my throat meets my neck
wondering will this be the day I finally bleed out and tell someone
I'm gay

being open was like a perfect match transfusion
a much-needed infusion of hope
a shot of freedom
and her affirmation a restoration of my very being
one down and a world to go
but within a day I was back to that place
anxiously, frantically, desperately searching for my pulse
hope and courage in full arrest
I put two fingers to my wrist
nothing
I checked that little indent where my throat meets my neck
nothing
I tried another finger
nothing
my other hand
nothing

god, please, tell me I'm still breathing
that I didn't risk it all for nothing
I feared ridicule and rejection, but not a killing
I opened the vein that I might finally live and love not die
that I might be filled, not emptied
that the constant pressure might be released, not drown me

the rain has ceased and I'm wet from tears
the gunman dead, yet not my fears
I survived one outing, can I face another

the worry like a body bag leaves me feeling smothered
a weight of grief keeps me still and desperate like Alejandro's or
Amanda's mother
needing to hear a ring, or feel a vibration
a pulse on my wrist, or that little indent where my throat meets my
neck
dear god, I don't care, I just need to feel it somewhere
however faint or weak, something, anything
just a pulse
I need to know
I'm here

Closets

in the back corner of the basement there was a plywood closet
with cobweb covered shelves and a string for a light switch
that was too high for me to reach without climbing or stretching on
my toes
more than once I was locked in it by the same hands that abused my
body
that left me terrified of intimacy and ashamed of sexuality

in the little blue bedroom upstairs
there was another closet filled with musty clothes
I used to hide in it
holding a flashlight tightly in my hands in case I needed it
there I learned to hate and shield my body

everywhere a closet
some of my own making, others built against my will
those childhood closets lock me in even still
keep me terrified and ashamed
my true self hidden and unnamed
the closet of today a grave yard just the same

two nights ago I took a first step toward life
told god and a saint I ain't ready to die
knowing that if I'm ever to live now is the time
I invited her in with a long anxious invitation
preceded by a nervous rambling explanation
that didn't come out as I'd rehearsed
but once she was in I came out
and said the words I thought I couldn't say aloud
I'm lesbian

she didn't run away
she held my hand
catching the salty tears on my cheek with acceptance and affirmation
I told her why now and some of what happened then
then I started rambling again
and kindly she listened again and again

long awaited, deathly afraid of words
spoken with and received in grace
after a prayer and tight embrace, I walked out to face a room with one
less person to fear
it felt like a light had been turned on that I wasn't quite able to reach
on my own
she climbed those rickety, rusty, cobweb covered shelves with me
and promised to be a part of the journey alongside me
yesterday
one step out of the closet, one step closer to authenticity

and today
I woke up ready to go back in
shut off the light and lock the door
even before my feet hit the floor a man went into a rainbow bar and
started shooting
more than 50 wounded and 49 are dead
this morning as my feet hit the annual conference floor I wanted to go
back in
turn off the lights and pad lock the door

they sang sweet songs
played a video highlighting the hate of the past debate
and said turn to your neighbor and discuss it once more
the woman next to me who smiled softly as she said
oh, we can't open up that door

I stepped out into a church, the source of my resurrection, my pay
check, my pension
that says you can't be in if you're out, if you're out go back in
a few might welcome you, while the loudest consider you sin
some of us will love and support you, while even more will say they do
only to remain silent when they're trying to try and crucify you

everything within me is screaming go back in
sure, it's dark and lonely in there, but you've adapted
found ways to catch glimpses of light and moments of fresh air
just stay, yes, it's dusty, damp, cold and uncomfortable, but it's safe in
there

and then I remembered
I'm only alive because I decided years ago that I couldn't stay in there
that I wouldn't define myself in those ways anymore
I'm more than the abuse I suffered, the violence I endured
I came out without a map or any real plan for a next step
but I took one and then a second and now here I am

I'm alive and want to live that way
I can't stay in there another day
I won't, I don't define myself that way anymore
I'm more than my sexuality
and my sexuality is far too valuable to be hid anymore
I come out again, without a map
fearful and hopeful for what's next

the light is on, the door is open and I'm out
breathing long and deep, praying hard and fast
god, as my feet hit the floor whatever may come
I'm out
keep me from opening the door and going back in
this morning, this afternoon, this evening, tomorrow and forever and
ever, amen

Unburdened and Unbent

woven between parables Luke helps us see Jesus
stopping his teaching to speak to her
nestled between a barren fig tree and an unlikely mustard seed she
stands
bent over and burdened
we don't know her age on this day
but we know for 18 years she's been this way
bent over and burdened

I wonder how she felt when Jesus calls her over
and says in front of an indignant crowd
"you're free, your suffering is over"

if you've ever been bent over for any length of time
you know it takes time to be comfortable standing up straight
if you've ever carried the weight of a burden in the depth of your
bones
you know it takes time to adjust to living without it

I used to go with my father on his chiropractic appointments
by the x-ray machine was a framed poster that read,
"as the twig is bent so goes the tree"
I always wondered what that meant
for years I asked anyone who would listen to me
not realizing my body was living out the answer

my spine and my mind, my heart and my soul
contorted and twisted and bent
by the neglectful, abusive, morbid soil of the vineyard where I'd been planted

and just after my 18th birthday I was spent
all that hunching over
all the ways I had to manipulate my way through the long days and sleepless nights
and I buckled

I wish Luke had given her a name and a voice
she never says a word
I'm sure she had something to say
women aren't bent over and burdened for no reason

and 18 years, that's a lifetime not a season
I wish Jesus had handed over the classroom and let her finish teaching

I imagine she would school the students
on both the physical and spiritual causes of her ailment
I imagine a beautiful, dynamic presentation
on the historical, political, and social implications of gender based
oppression
and I hear her deliver a challenging and compassionate lesson
on female spinal compression also described as being burdened and
bent over

I have a name though not everyone knows or uses it
sometimes I'm too filled with fear and shame to use it myself
I often go for the seat in the back of the room
or to the last pew in the sanctuary and sit hunched over
I learned this behavior early as routinely as I visited the chiropractor with my father

don't speak up, don't cry, don't make a fuss
and whatever you do
don't dare reveal the secrets of the house
silence made me and kept me burdened and bent over

I'm glad that Jesus called out the hypocrisy of the crowd
for caring more about sabbath rules than her need for healing
I'm glad that in the end the crowd could rejoice in the moral lesson of
his teaching
but wouldn't this have been the perfect time to ask her to speak
to give her name
to name her pain and the consequences of it
to share the origins of it
to hear from the crowd and the leaders an apology

I'm grateful for those in the church today
who call out our hypocritical ways
I'm grateful for those who dare to say
that our obsession with rules and discipline bends and burdens the gospel
but I just keep thinking about all of those suffering from the church's need for
healing
who don't get to speak or give their names

or name their pain and the consequences of it
or share the origins of it
or hear from bishops, superintendents, pastors, leaders and members an apology

what was it like for her to walk away from the synagogue and the crowd
from the one that healed her
presumably alone, putting one foot in front of the other
no longer bent over, standing tall
did she feel proud
what else did she feel
while the burden may have changed I imagine it didn't go completely away
set free from some demons
probably thankful for her first round of healing
perhaps anxiously waiting to the receive the next
unbending, unburdening is a process, not a one-time event

I don't know what life will be like after I walk away from the church and the process
and while I will always be thankful for the church of my birth
that offered me my first round of healing
that's exactly why I can't stay
because as long as I'm here silent and submissive there won't be a next
as long as I'm here defending my worth
the hard work that goes into being able to stand tall and unbent is being undone

It's such a weird place to be
like between a barren vineyard filled with fruitless fig trees
and the promise of a mustard seed
knowing that the church that gave me the courage
to name and claim who I am also says that who I am is not okay

some say,
you're gay, that overrides everything, nothing else matters now, you can't stay
I'm not walking away because of them

others say, the moral arc of the universe is bending toward justice
just wait, the commission is coming, a new bishop is coming
it simply has to change, who you are doesn't matter
don't admit you're practicing and everything will be okay
we'll protest and protect you, you have to stay

I can't stay to appease and avoid disappointing them
or to give them another cause to fight for

and there are those who refuse to say anything
for fear, for cowardliness, for the preservation of a mythical centrism they stay quiet
sadly, this silent majority speaks the loudest

I can't stay
I'm leaving for my healing
not because of the messianic demands placed on clergy
or the inequitable compensation
or the system's exploitation and fascination with gimmicks, gurus and growth tracks
or the continued silence in the face of rising racism, sexism, classism
and general hatred in our society
or the sinful way we've reduced healthy sexual ethics to hetero-monogamy

I'm leaving for my healing
at 18 I gave in to heavy burdens
resigned myself to bent over living
removed myself from community believing the lies
that like splintered twigs were used to beat me into surrender
I've spent the last 20 years learning to stand
to live, to love, to walk
and my next step
is to hand in my resignation
to surrender my credentials
so that finally
I can proudly speak my name
and boldly name my pain
and confidently claim my healing from it
and then get on with it
with living, and loving, and walking upright
unburdened
unbent
and planting mustard seeds
in vineyards that systems deem undeserving
proving that bent twigs don't always kill the tree

{Advent}

taught to surrender, to lay it all at the altar, to come just as you are, to
leave empty and unrecognizable, to pour out your soul, to be filled up
later, to confess your sins
to name the things that tempt you
your will, your ambitions, your desires, your flesh
to bind the things that test you
your fears, your tears, your insecurities, your thinking, your dreaming
surrender it all, all that god gave you, all that makes you uniquely you

the trees in my yard are living in perilous times in these last days of
October
green leaves fighting to maintain their color and identity
red, orange, yellow tightly hanging on in hopes of staying connected to
the branches
are they resisting surrender, delaying the inevitable
do they know that snow is coming, as is a cold November
do they remember last year and all the years before
are they conscious enough to even care

while human eyes admire autumn beauty and muse about transitions,
singing the wonders of creation, do the leaves and trees think at all
about changing seasons
do they participate voluntarily or is surrender an annual painful journey

my life began and ended in autumn's span
I was born just before her September arrival and I died in mid-October
as I watched the color fade on the face of the one whose twisted love
raised me
and held the hand that violently betrayed me as her chest fell for the
last time
outside the moonlight hovered over burnt wet leaves as the wind
hallowed through barren, naked trees

this year, 23 years later I'm rethinking fall's meaning and the purpose
of surrender
maybe Sarah McLachlan and John Denver know better, there is
something sweet about it
maybe it's the church that makes it so bitter

this whole notion of original sin, that we are inherently evil
in need of salvation even before we leave the womb
this belief that we are tainted and soiled and only a bath in blood with
cleanse us
that an innocent man had to die, publicly humiliated and crucified, to
redeem us
no wonder we are bound
and after singing surrender for more than 2,000 years
still far more lost than found

I'm not naïve enough to think an institution is going to change its
foundation
no matter how cracked and shifted it might be
I'm not foolish enough to think that the church will alter its position
on the human condition no matter how unholy it may be
so this fall I'm preparing to pour myself a new foundation, changing
my position on what it means to be me

what if my will and self-ambition and desires and flesh aren't
temptations but gifts
my fears and tears, insecurities, thoughts and dreams are reason for
hope and not regret

what if the trees are a model to follow and the leaves an example to
pattern
what if in deliberately choosing to let go and reveal my full self
I find joy and meaning intentionally embracing the long coming winter
and facing the numbing cold I find that long sought-after healing

what if the drive to the bishop's office is like the long walk down the
sanctuary aisle to the altar but better, sweet and not bitter
each step marked by power rather than shame and the courage to keep
moving pushes out the pain, and the strength to surrender allows me
to hold my head up high all the way
to maintain my dignity when I say
today, I voluntarily surrender my credentials
this is of my own choice and choosing, to humbly, confidently confess
that for your hypocrisy you are losing and tragically you have lost so
many

28

I surrender a life of silence so that I can live into god's will that I
would have life abundantly and live authentically
I surrender a life of secrets so that I am free to love and serve
ambitiously
I surrender the need to have the church validate my identity so that I
can dance with pride and without the fear of charges of incompatibility
I surrender the notion that only straight desires are sacred and holy

I'm not yielding to fear, but releasing it
I'm not resigning to a long night of tears, but learning from it
I'm not giving into insecurity, but boldly facing it
I'm not abandoning my conviction, but claiming it
I'm not relinquishing my dream, but waking into it

the sun has set since I sat down to write
for the night I cannot see any trees or distinguish one color leaf from
another
even the moon is hidden
they are calling for a storm
change is coming, transition leaves me anxious
the barren trees and brittle leaves leave my restless
and strangely not hopeless

I've waited my whole life for this
I died for this
the chance to surrender
not to become, but to fall gently into
to finally love and accept all that I am and am created to be
I surrender self-hatred and shame to at long last celebrate me

Letter to the Bishop

I write to share a painful, yet hope-filled decision, one born after a long dark night of suffering and revealed in the anticipation that better things are yet to come for me and the denomination that I so love.

Since I was a young girl, running through the halls and sanctuary aisles of the church, Advent has been my favorite liturgical season. Even when I did not fully understand all that Christians are waiting for, the anticipation was exciting and deepened my faith and desire to know more about the things of God. Certainly, there had to be more to life than our suffering.

More to life than the economic struggles plaguing the city of my birth. More to life than the seemingly endless cycle of poverty and unemployment affecting my family.
More to life than the physical and mental illness afflicting my loved ones.
More to life than the abuse and depression that left me crying out to God for relief.

The United Methodist Church has always been my "something more" and never was this so obvious as during Advent.

The sanctuary where I was baptized and confirmed, where I first received and served Holy Communion, the Sunday school classrooms where I learned the Bible and Wesleyan theology and hymns, the basement choir room where I fell in love with handbells, the Commons where I roller-skated and played shuffleboard and the stage where I donned a donkey costume and danced for the Christmas pageant—all spaces and opportunities that provided safety, refuge, and acceptance year round for the formative years of my life. But during Advent especially these places and the faces that tended to them burned even brighter with the lights of hope, love, peace, joy, and the Christ Child.

Today another Advent season begins. Though geographically I am in a new place, my community still suffers. The people of Detroit, like our kin in Flint, wait for clean affordable water, restoration of democracy, quality education, access to employment, transportation and the benefits of development, and an end to racialized violence and oppression. This Advent more than any other I am reminded of the similarities of suffering in present day American cities and the villages and towns spread across the Galilee some 2,000 years ago.

I begin this Advent season as a provisional deacon, called to ministries of word, service, justice, and compassion. For two years I have given my all in service with survivors of the August 11, 2014 flood, the largest disaster in the country for that year, leaving more than 44,000 families in northwest Detroit alone under water.

Despite the lack of attention from government and municipalities, media, and even the United Methodist Church, the project has risen above the muck to offer hope, healing, and recovery to families who have waited two years for assistance.

These two years navigating the mold and debris of flooded basements, some of which have not had working furnaces since the flood, have left me longing for hope. Hope for those individuals and families left to recover on their own. Hope for my own life and future.

The Christian tradition has long been marked by dualism, confronted by contrasting forces competing for our loyalty and attention.

We would not anticipate hope if despair were not a reality.
We would not long for love if hate were not so prominent.
We would not seek peace if conflict did not persist.
We would not ache for joy if sorrow did not surround us.
We would not prepare for the coming Christ Child if creation reflected the belovedness God intended.

I would not write this letter if the United Methodist Church made room for all at the table of grace and at the Christ Child's cradle of love and light.

After years of faithfulness and hard work in the provisional process, I am due to submit my ordination questions to the Board of Ordained Ministry in January 2017 and go before the Board for interviews in March. However, rather than submitting answers to the ordination questions, in January following the completion of the flood recovery project, I will surrender my credentials. I will not seek full membership as an ordained United Methodist deacon.

After great preparation and waiting, I am able to proudly say and boldly claim that I am lesbian. To deny my sexuality any longer, to continue hiding who I am, to engage with the United Methodist Church in a game of "don't ask-don't tell" would be a betrayal of the long journey leading me to this difficult and beautiful self realization. The despair, hate, conflict, and sorrow that I have faced on the journey to self acceptance would be given rights to return should I stay in a system that values law over love, rules above grace, and institutional preservation over the sacred worth of her children. What will be said of a system that will baptize, confirm, and ordain her children, but then cut them off from the body when they dare to be themselves? What would be said of me, if I remained in a system that applauds my ministry with those on the margins of society and awards me for my commitment to justice, but that also demands I stay silent about the ways I am bound by the chains of injustice it places on my body and spirit?

Over the coming days and weeks of Advent, I am committed to intentional prayer for my future and that of our beloved United Methodist Church. While the decision to surrender my credentials and not seek ordination has been affirmed in many ways, it certainly does not come without deep pain and sorrow. The grief is palpable. It is the anticipation of a brighter, more authentic, non-anxious life that sustains me. Ironically, becoming spiritually, emotionally, and physically healthy and finding the courage to accept who I am has resulted in great loss, not the least of which is my hard-earned place among clergy and my God given call to the ministry of deacon in the United Methodist Church. Yet, there are also gains. I anticipate the day when I can wake and proudly say who I am and who I love without fear of judgment, punishment, and trial. I preferred to live out my call in the United Methodist Church, but my call to word, service, justice, and compassion will not end with the surrender of my credentials. I wait for God to reveal exactly how and where I will be in ministry next.

As leaders in the Annual Conference, I ask that you too intentionally pray for the future of our church during this Advent season. The

United Methodist Church is losing. We are suffering for the loss of gifted and called clergy, talented and committed laity. We are losing our relevance and credibility. We are losing sight of our mission, of God's mission. What do we gain by discriminating against LGBTQIA individuals? What is won when we prosecute clergy who practice radical inclusion and hospitality? What is the future of a denomination born and bathed in grace and now drowning and dying in hateful condemnation?

And so, like the people of the Galilee living under Roman occupation, we wait.
Like the thirsty citizens of Flint, we wait.
Like the flood survivors of Detroit, we wait.
Like a country in the midst of division, we wait.
Like a world in need of healing, we wait.
As a denomination adrift, we wait.
We wait for hope, love, joy, and peace.
We anticipate the birth of the Christ Child and the dawning of God's beloved community.

I anticipate the full inclusion of LGBTQIA individuals in the United Methodist Church, but in the meantime, I voluntarily surrender my credentials, as I refuse to surrender my dignity and pride while you debate my worth.

Bishop, I welcome an opportunity to meet with you to share more about this heart wrenching and liberating decision.

Gracefully, Peacefully, Hope-fully yours,

Rev. Rebecca Wilson

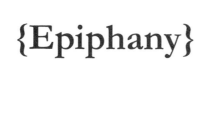

{Epiphany}

Mangos

the greatest preacher I'd known didn't speak to me from a pulpit with
a bible in her hand, but from a sofa in a Border's café, holding a
notebook, reading poetry she wrote about home in another country,
the sights, sounds, scents and flavors of her culture

I've met a lot of ministers, but none quite like her
it's not her standing behind a table, serving bread and juice that I
remember, but us sitting at her kitchen table together
an invitation to eat rice and yogurt with my fingers
it was different and didn't come natural, but still felt comfortable

she was the first to ever offer me a mango
I had no idea how to peel it, let alone eat it
sweet juice ran down my chin and the pulp stuck under my nails
she was the first female pastor we had, that alone made me admire her
and think maybe I, too, could be something special

when it was time to move into the parsonage,
I offered to help unpack boxes, yet worried she wouldn't want my help
I was 22, unemployed, depressed, pumped full of prozac, suicidal, and
a chain smoker
she accepted my offer
and passed no judgment when I stood in the driveway to take a drag
every half an hour

the first poem I shared with her was about communion, how I felt
unworthy to receive it
she told me to keep writing, that god loved me even if I didn't feel it
she didn't seem like someone who would lie
so I kept writing, praying, wanting desperately to believe it
that god could love me

five generations of my family worshipped there
most had died or moved away before she came, a lot had changed
since I was little
like my family, most of congregation too had died or moved away
and not long after she came, those who stayed decided they would
rather die than risk real change

37

they thought church was a place to drive to for an hour on Sunday
and then lock the doors before heading to lunch on the way back
home in the suburbs
where they cast condemnation on the city that funded their middle
class dream
any thought of letting in people of another culture, race or income
bracket
was cause for more locks, bars and gates
and soon they voted to close
by ballot box, I lost my church, the one safe place I'd known
the one place I felt welcome or anything close to special or like home

there was a final service with lots of guests, tradition and communion
I had hoped they'd let her preach, a poem or one of her captivating
sermons
but no, she didn't get much of a role
when the service was over she packed up the parsonage and moved
south
and my life slid further downhill, and I didn't see her for years
I thought I'd never step foot in a church again
or find another minister who would dare to say that god loved me
and invite me to believe it

I imagine her surprise all those years later when I called
asking if I could come see her
I'd gotten my life together
was working in a church, finishing college, applying to seminary
I'd quit smoking, was living without medication and hadn't been
hospitalized in years
I wanted to be a preacher and preach like her, in words and ways
people could connect to
I wanted to be a minister and minister like her
offering people a meal they never tried before
helping them see god in ways they never considered before
following Jesus to places they never walked before
alongside people they never encountered before
loving themselves, believing in themselves like they never could before
I wanted to serve the church in such a way that would open doors and
not close them
that wouldn't leave hopeless people without a sanctuary
without a space to gather

I'm feeling a lot like I felt after that final service
like I lost my best friend
this time the church isn't closing, but my time serving it is
years of training and testing and preaching and praying didn't prepare me for this
for having to choose between living my truth and living in fear
it was an impossible choice, but truth won out, and honesty has cost me everything

the church that baptized, confirmed, and commissioned me, and appoints me
now requires me to leave
they'll tell the story differently, but in the end
I passed every test, answered every question, met every requirement but one
I'm out because I'm lesbian

I saw her tonight and as we sat around a table the memory of that meal simmers so strong
I taste the rice and the yogurt and feel it on my fingertips
the mango juice dripping down my chin and the pulp under my nails
reminding me, god does love me, even if I can't feel it
that I gave my all and have nothing to be ashamed of, even if it seems like it
that there will be new ways to minister even if the pain is too deep to believe it
that church may fail and disappoint and betray us, but there can be life outside it
that all things are possible
that rice and yogurt can sustain us
and that those mangos just might save us
if and when we try them

On Birth Canals and Rocks

there was no one waiting outside your mother's birth canal to give you a rock,
said the man at the podium presenting a resolution urging us to
recognize the unborn baby in the womb as fully human from the
moment of conception

but what if there were?
a person, an usher, a greeter, a team of colorful cheerleaders, a choir of
angels waiting outside your mother's birth canal to give you a rock

o, precious one here is a rock
smooth like silk, clear like crystal
gentle like warm water from a fountain
warm like a burning bush on a holy mountain
cool like a Lake Michigan spring evening breeze
healing like a strawberry shortcake band aid on a freshly scraped knee

o, beautiful blessed little one here is a rock for you to cling to in weary
lands
when the church says you're incompatible
when you're living on the streets
because your parents' pastor preaches that you're an abomination
when border patrol turns you away
when ICE locks you in a cage
when police officers shoot you as you raise your hands to say, *I am not
armed*
when a judge sentences you to life for a non-violent crime
when you haven't had dinner for the third night in a row
when you cower in a corner as a swat team raids your home
when you're coughing up a lung
and can't go to a doctor because your insurance was cut off months
ago
when you walk to school past abandoned homes alone and do your
best to learn mathematics without books or pencils or even a seat of
your own
when you decide to stand up and speak against a nation
overtaken by old white men in red hats and expensive suits
who used your mother's birth canal to corral more power and amass
more wealth

while the resolution urging us to recognize the unborn baby in the
womb as fully human from the moment of conception didn't pass
it certainly moved me
inspired me to live a life of giving rocks in a world where the majority
are throwing stones

there was no one waiting outside your mother's birth canal to give you
a rock
what if there were?

A Map

The Goonies. Maybe you're familiar with this 1980s movie? A group of teenagers are spending their last weekend together. Their homes are being foreclosed so developers can build a golf course. Mikey, like the rest of the Goonies, is a misfit. His dad is the curator of a museum and their attic is filled with rejected artifacts. Rummaging through these unwanted items, they come across a treasure map from the 1600s.

Mikey recounts the story of pirate One-Eyed Willy. After stealing a treasure, the British Armada sails after him. Willy sails his ship into a cave to hide. The British find them and blow up the walls all around them. For years Willy and his crew are in the cave hiding their treasures and setting booby traps to keep future looters away. Story has it that in the end Willy killed all his men.

Chunk, one of the Goonies gang says, "Wait, if he killed all his men how did the map or the story get out?"

Mikey replies, "My dad said one of the guys must have gotten out with the map."

This is my hope for today. That some way the map and the story will get out. That somehow you will leave here thinking differently about our denomination's exclusion of LGBTQ individuals in the life of the church. The ability to stand before you and say that I am lesbian is the culmination of a 20-year story of struggle and grace.

Last year's Annual Conference is a significant chapter in my story. I presented about the Flood Recovery Project. I put on a Tyvek suit, gloves, goggles, and a respirator in hopes of getting people excited about coming to Detroit to muck out basements. Shortly before putting on this outfit, I took off a mask. I told a friend that I am lesbian and that I was afraid. Afraid because in finally accepting who God made me to be, I wasn't sure how I could remain in a system that says who God made me to be is incompatible with our teachings. I didn't say it out loud, but I knew then that I couldn't stay.

The next morning, we heard news of the Orlando Pulse Nightclub shooting. 49 people killed. Another 50 wounded. I couldn't say it out loud, but I knew then that I couldn't stay. We were given slips of paper and asked to write questions or concerns on the decision of General Conference to call for a special commission on Human Sexuality. I wasn't going to write it, but I knew then that I couldn't stay.

We were asked to turn to our neighbor and discuss human sexuality. My neighbor very kindly said, "I don't talk about these things." I wouldn't say it out loud, but I knew then that I couldn't stay. I am fully aware there are ways I could stay. But for me these ways are incompatible with healthy, authentic, faithful living.

My ministry has been about advocating for and working with people, communities, and churches on the margins. My position allowed me to work closely with our city churches, many staffed by less than full time pastors, living offering to offering, and carrying wounds of past appointments and disappointments. Here I learned new lessons about the treasures of the church. These churches were essential to the success of the Flood Recovery Project. These churches don't have diamonds and rubies. Their financial situation keeps them on the brink of closure, but their faith and generosity is wealth of a far more valuable kind.

My ministry unexpectedly became advocacy for flood survivors. People forsaken after the largest disaster of the year. I was in and out of flood-ravaged basements, homes that went two winters without working heat. I traveled the state and the country telling this story. Begging for funds and volunteers. Challenging FEMA and local government about the lack of attention and the dire need for resources. All the while knowing that I was employed by an institution that enjoyed the fruits of my ministry, but would cut me off if they knew who I was. A system that praised my advocacy for others and shared my pictures and stories freely, but would silence me if I ever advocated for my own full inclusion.

After successfully navigating tunnels and booby traps, the Goonies find Willy's ship and all the rich stuff. In part because of stories left behind by failed explorers who went before them. Through a small opening they escape the cave with just enough jewels to save their homes from foreclosure.

The United Methodist Church is a lot like Willy's ship. We've sailed into a cave and the walls are blowing up around us. Our gifts are not reaching the world and the world's gifts cannot reach us. When the Goonies found Willy's skeleton he was surrounded by treasure. His hands full of pearls, sapphires, and emeralds. I stand before you with hands full of emotion.

I am angry. I am grieving. I am baffled by the fact that the church that baptized, confirmed, and commissioned me; that would have soon ordained me; that guided me away from an abusive family; that introduced me to the woman who would become my mother; and that gave me the courage to love and accept myself is now breaking my heart in ways I didn't know possible. And I am hopeful. Anticipating a future not marked by self-hatred and fear. Looking forward to new ways of living out my call.

I've been a misfit most of my life. Circumstances left me on the outside looking in. Being on the inside for the first time, in my ministry I was committed to looking out. To seeking out those on the margins and inviting them in. I used to pray, God, use me in spite of my misfit status. Sadly, it's in surrendering my credentials that I finally realize my painful experiences on the margins are a gift and not a liability. Maybe it's a misfit who will lead the church out of its dark cave and into a new day? This new day will only dawn when we tell the whole story. Not just the hopeful chapters, but also those depicting the anger, grief, and hypocrisy.

I am reminded of another group of misfits. We might not be here today if they hadn't persisted in sharing the story and the map that goes with it. Jesus' followers didn't hide out in a cave after his death. Nor did they only tell the story of his resurrection. They shared it all. His birth in a barn. His childhood on the run. His betrayal. His confrontations with leaders. His violent crucifixion. There is no Easter without Good Friday. No new birth without a death.

It's hard to imagine my life without the United Methodist Church, but I will find my way. It's also hard to imagine the United Methodist future. If there is a united future it will come from the stories of faithful LGBTQ clergy and laity told in our own voices. And from the voices of leaders as willing to risk their credentials as they are to receive them from those forced to make this impossible decision.

It only takes one person for a story to get out. It only takes a few hands to turn a ship around. Hands full of faith and grace are worth far more than hands full of gold and silver. In handing you my credentials, I offer you a map, symbolizing my hope and my prayer, that you will steer us in a new way.

{Lent}

Face Value

right before I left, a decision I deeply grieve and do not regret
a district superintendent said around a crowded table
we thank god for you, for who you were, who you are, who you are becoming
I didn't see that one coming, obviously neither did he
in my dreams and nightmares
my brightest and darkest moments those words still come at me
they come for me, uninvited, unwelcomed
knocking me over like the hypocrisy of this reality

sorry, now that we know you're a lesbian
and unwilling to publicly profess that you're not practicing nothing else matters
now that you're out and not down for becoming a poster child
or putting your life on parade or display, sorry, there's no place for you
the trophies awarded you, the praise given you, the ministry entrusted you, the grace
baptized you, the credentials commissioned you, the faith placed in you, the thanks
offered to god for you
none of it matters

my grandpa cautioned us kids to never write on a dollar bill or rip it
any mark, any tear, he said, will cause it to lose its value
maybe my grandpa and my church went to the same school
the one that teaches students how to judge, how to calculate worth
how to seek and find the specks in others' eyes
while justifying and rationalizing the log in your own

it feels like it, but mostly I know I'm not alone
there's this woman, we've never met, but I feel like I know her
the subject of poems and songs, and prayers and sermons
everyone's got an opinion about her
her worth, how she values herself and her prized possession
she's unnamed, known only as the sinful woman
and the way the story is written a woman's sin is always sexual
but these are lies told to shame us even deeper

do you see her? she stands behind him weeping
do you hear her? falling to her knees weeping even louder
do you feel her? her tears a cleansing balm
her hair a heated drying towel

her perfumed oil the most precious thing she owned
and without reservation or hesitation she pours it out upon his feet

then right in step
these men who have just witnessed this selfless, sacred, sacrificial gift
begin a debate about money
what it's really worth
and about debt, when it's forgivable, when it's not
when it's okay to judge, when it's not
did she feel like I did

I'm sitting there crying
telling you what for years I was too ashamed and too afraid to say
that I'm lesbian, preparing to give up everything I've ever known and
wanted
because I know that in living authentically this sanctuary is no longer
safe for me
all I was asking was that you offer, not a jar full, but just a drop of
grace to me
and all you could say,
*are you sure you don't want to rewrite your letter to specify specifically that you're
not practicing?*
*are you certain you don't want to sign away your privacy, your last ounce of dignity,
and be edited into my documentary?*

Jesus, in one of his last encounters
having recovered from the ill-timed financial debate
saves the best for last
go in peace, he tells her, *your faith has saved you*
it's faith, not laws or discipline that saves us
it's god, not human currencies or institutions that value us
it's hard to remember this these days when every answer is no
and with all the doors that still stay closed
but they were wrong about her, about a lot of things
she wasn't the problem or a sin

sometimes people don't know to respond
when a determined woman knows what she's been called to do and
does it
her life, her being, her oil anointed long before she poured it out

grandpa was wrong too, about me, about women and money
sometimes that marking, that scribble
that tear in the corner of the dollar bill makes it worth more
why else did he leave us a coffee can full of copper pennies and buffalo
nickels and say
keep these, someday they'll be worth more than face value

the coins in my hands are cold, but my feet are warm
I feel her, her oil poured out
I hear her, reminding me, *there is a place, a space for you*
I see her, preparing it
there's a sweet smell in the air leading me to it
I believe god
help me to believe it

Thirsty

you don't realize how thirsty you are
until you sit down to spit into a plastic tube
the DNA kit instructions say
no smoking, eating or drinking for 30 minutes before giving a sample
I hadn't thought about water all day, but suddenly I was so thirsty
I couldn't think of anything other than how bad I wanted a drink of
water

a cup, a glass, a mug, a pitcher of who I was and where I went
I wish it were that simple
a drip, a drop, a leak, a drizzle of who I am and where I'm going
I wish it weren't so painful
god, I am so thirsty and nothing can quench me

DNA, the scientific words I cannot say, but ancestry says
for $99 they'll make my spit holler the story hidden in my genes
though still unwritten the results will likely read
irish, english, norwegian, and in a not so shocking revelation
reveal one of my great-great grandmothers wasn't fully caucasian

but what I'm really thirsty for and what my spit won't tell
is where I must go to find myself
there was no box to check to get directions on how to reconnect
myself
cause when I wasn't looking I went missing
have you seen me
I left years ago in search of water and of answers to questions I
couldn't ask

that tree as thirsty as Jesus was
cut down and cut up so he could be nailed up on it
that tree uprooted and disconnected like he was
struggling to breathe, dying just like he was
thirsty for a drink of water and of answers
what have they done to us, what will become of us

that soldier of the empire crucifying him on that tree manipulated into
a cross

is he one of us
he did offer him a drink when no one else would

are we supposed to be grateful when systems responsible for publicly
humiliating us
torturing us and ultimately killing us
apply a small drip of water to our parched bleeding lips right before
they bury us
that's a bitter drink to swallow, for Jesus and for us who long to follow
in his footsteps

like Jesus and the tree and his enemies I'm thirsty
for people who pour out honesty and filter out hypocrisy
who will quit patronizing and straight-plaining me
stop quoting scripture and the book of discipline to me
and will celebrate who I am and just be glad that I'm this close to
finding me

on a cold, dark, rainy Friday morning I drove hours
to walk through an old cemetery full of even older trees
searching for graves of old relatives I didn't know existed before I spit
into that tube

Madge and Clara, Sarah and Hannah
women long since gone that I'd give anything to meet
I imagine their stories quenching me
helping me understand where I come from and where I went
cause when I wasn't looking, I went away, believing that who I was
wasn't okay
that my very being was a mistake, that the only way to atone was to live
a lie

and while I didn't find all the graves I was hoping for I spotted my
missing self
standing near a tall wide evergreen, rooted and connected to the
creation around me
drinking from the beauty, the history, the mystery surrounding me
I was too afraid to walk over and talk to me

I'd like to offer me a drink

a cup of apology for having left myself so thirsty
a glass of healing balm for having wounded me
a mug of love for having hated me
a pitcher of kisses for having betrayed me, far more than three times
a fountain flowing with second chances for having crucified me

maybe today is not the day for us to meet and to speak
maybe today is meant for grieving and repenting
and spitting out all the poison I ingested when there was no clean
water to be had
maybe today is not the day for drinking or for seeking answers
maybe today it's okay to just be sad
maybe today is meant for sitting under rooted trees just asking
questions
and for being unashamed and fearlessly thirsty

but come Sunday, oh, Sunday anything is possible
a lot can happen in 3 days
dead trees bearing fruit, stones rolling away
tombs emptying, bodies rising

is this reality or a sign that I'm delirious from years of being thirsty
thirsty for water and answers
mostly just thirsty for me

Forsaken

it's hard to feel forsaken
why have you forsaken me

I dared to be who I was made to be
to live the love inside of me
I did what I was called to do
I walked the path you led me to
I said and I prayed the words I was inspired to
god, not by some strange mythical being, but by you
damn it, I couldn't feel this forsaken if I didn't really believe in you
so why, tell me why you left
show me where you went
if I didn't feel so angry and abandoned
I'd run right for you and demand an explanation

eli, eli, lama sabachthani

I've heard these words, read these words for years
but never felt them quite like this
the betrayal, the humiliation, the shame
your life, the dice in someone else's game
cast, cast aside like a lot, it hurts a whole whole lot,
to know your side of the story has not been told
that a room of colleagues took a vote
to confirm your leaving and negate your humanity
and you were uninvited, told a vote was not required
I probably would not have come, but I should have been invited
yeah, I heard you when you said I should have asked more questions
but I was breathless and dying and naively still too trusting
surely at least one of you was being honest

it's hard to see another sitting comfortably in your seat at the table
your plate and cup scrubbed clean of your name and your memory

it's hard to hear the excuses and platitudes of those who raise their
hands in resignation
when just last week their hands were lifted in celebration
congratulating you on a job well done

it's hard to taste your own bitter tears formed from the rejection of not your enemies
but rather your most beloved friends and peers
the ones who made your suffering all about them
like a sponge full of vinegar when all you requested was a sip of water

it's hard to touch your own burning flesh caught fire by another's wrath
when you summoned the courage to ask them why
why they left you alone in the cold and they replied
the truth, we just forgot you

oh the pain, so deep, so raw
the flames, the heat, so intense, so consuming you're left unrecognizable
paralyzed by the sting, the slow acting agony

it's hard to feel forsaken
because the natural inclination is to ask why
why
but the answer to this impossible question can never be healing
it's like the instinct to say goodbye
all those notes and letters and no replies
I should have left it alone
instead of finding closure, I found myself more alone
more forsaken
if that's even possible

it's hard to feel forsaken
to just sit with it, not to intellectualize or rationalize it
I've obviously failed at not poeticizing it
it's hard to feel forsaken

but today it's all there is to do
to be
to feel
it's hard to be forsaken

why god, my god, why

Were You There

were you there
no, I wasn't in the room when they voted yes
we affirm your call to ministry
because I was in another state graduating from seminary

and no, I wasn't in the room three years later
when they voted yes
we accept your surrendered credentials
because I was told that decision didn't require a vote
and because I was at home on spiritual life support

but I am here today
although not in the ball room
because my dance card is the wrong color
it's pink, not white or yellow or green
but you know, really, I have always been something in between

I'm outside alone sitting on a picnic bench crying
between a rock and a soft place
tears of unbearable grief, unbelievable relief
of course, I am thinking about the votes
how could I not
for a people who discourage gambling
we sure make a lot of decisions by casting lots
we seem to have forgot
all the people we cast away
before we won the courage to play this high-stake game
I can be happy for them and sad for me
that's what it means to finally be free

my attendance isn't counted
my presence isn't wanted
and yes, I am here today
and I feel grace saying
me too, I'm here living outside the established bar with you

{Easter}

Mary Magdalene

she's been my Mary Magdalene
a presence even when I've tried to hide from it
present when I needed to feel it
when in my weakness I needed to lean on it
love in the flesh when for my humanness I needed to touch it
compassion personified when for my shame I needed to sit close and
breathe it
courage for when my fear took hold and I needed to embrace it

she's been my Mary Magdalene
she was there
early on
when the day was at its bleakest
aware of and familiar with the place
preparing and praying over the space
finding and reflecting grace
polishing stones with her grace
revealing their hidden worth
they were gems underneath

she's been my Mary Magdalene
the reason I'm not in a grave
the reason I'm not rolled up and wrapped in oiled, soiled death linens
she stood with me and she stood for me
she sat with me and she sat for me
her shoulder held my head when I wept
and she wept with and she wept for me
she met the demons in my head
and the ones sitting on my feet haunting me and binding me
and they said to her
"why are you here? this one you hold is shameful. worthless. broken.
let her go."

and she said to them
"no. you've taken all you will from her. now, you go!"

and in disbelief I asked her
"why are you here? why do you care? how could you love one like me?"

and she pointed her finger to the garden and said,
"because of them."
she's been my Mary Magdalene
reminding me that gardeners are angels and saviors in disguise
reminding me that because they live, she lives and so do I

she's been my Mary Magdalene
introducing me over and over again to our teacher
reminding me that our teacher, a friend and a healer
knows my name and calls me by it
even when, especially when, I don't know who I am or what to call myself

she's been my Mary Magdalene
speaking life
so clearly and honestly, how could I not hear it

modeling life
so simply and sincerely, how could I not see it

preaching good news
with conviction and so boldly, how could I not believe it

she's been my Mary Magdalene
the reason that after three days of grief and despair
and a lifetime of waiting to die I'm not there

she's been my Mary Magdalene
leading me to a garden blooming with wisdom
from both of them I'm learning
learning when to let go and what to hold on to

she's been my Mary Magdalene
pronouncing life and blessing over me, saying
"I want you to see what I do. today you are the one that Jesus loves."

In Circles

in a circle, we created a circle
chairs with plush cushions perfectly arranged in a sterile office space
an altar in the center to help center this merciless moment on this most
unholy occasion

in a circle, we sat, in a circle
the sadness palpable, grief indescribable
I cannot describe the shame that burned my throat each time that I
swallowed
in a circle, we sang, in a circle
I don't remember the chorus, only the way our position divided us
us and them, supporters and those who would claim to be and then
me, soon to be neither

in a circle, we stood silent, in a circle
a collision of full cabinets and empty closets
the bishop was silent as I handed over my title, my papers, my
credentials
in a circle, I surrendered, in a circle
I said what I could, far too much and oh so little, I only hope that it
mattered
does it matter to anyone that I made the best of the worst decision
possible
to surrender my hopes, my dreams, myself, all that the Spirit ordered
because someone somewhere decided my sexuality's a sin
that a woman loving a woman cancels her gifts

in a circle, I stifled my tears, in a circle
because I feared if I cried I'd drown in the waters
and the pharisees would cite some ancient law as reason not to save
me
in a circle, I left my heart, my call, seemingly my all, in a circle
in a circle, we prayed, in a circle
it tasted bitter and it felt hollow as a clanging symbol

in a circle, we created, a circle
that was more octagonal than round and we sat on whatever could be found
chairs or the stairs, or a table
rainbow colored curtains served as the altar centering us all in this most merciful moment

in a circle, we sat, in a circle
the bishop shared how he overcame his fears
to become pastor to those on the streets dying of AIDS
how he built beds for the homeless, gave hope to the hopeless
how he still dreams of one he couldn't save
remembering the blood dripping from her veins, who despite finding welcome and love
couldn't out run the shame and her name sounded like mine

in a circle, we sang, in a circle
a divine harmonized chorus, spanish, english, no language could divide us
powerfully the spirit united us as we sang all together in zulu
when christ is present there is no estados unidos or mexico, methodist or catholic

in a circle, we stood silent, in a circle
as one by one they spoke, telling their own story in their own voice
how the church welcomed them when their family rejected them
how they found home and hope and purpose leading worship and workshops for others
how depression was lifted when their worth was uplifted
how grief lessened when comforted
how shame was erased when their full self-acknowledged
how everything changed when their calling was celebrated and their gifts were accepted

in a circle, I surrendered, in a circle
from my seat on the marble step I lay it all down
the lies I was told and wrongly believed, the time spent deceived
I am not a sin or a result of another's
the only abomination the years and the love I lost to self-hatred
in a circle, I started to cry, in a circle

yes, I was afraid, yet I wasn't the only one and I knew if I fell someone
would catch me

in a circle, I reheard my calling, in a circle
I never quite knew what to do with titles or papers or credentials
robes and stoles and cinctures
I simply wanted to offer compassion to those on the margin as I knew
that place so well
and tell stories of resurrection, they don't just happen in heaven
and to help bring forth justice in a world that's not so
and to serve all god's children, as Jesus said, go

in a circle, we prayed, in a circle
and it tasted like aqua de sandia and fresh tortillas
and even with the noise of engines revving in the street it sounded like
shalom
in a circle, I heard god's voice again, in a circle calling
your calling, you did not, you could not, surrender your calling
I'm calling, still, be still, rest in my hand, as you prepare for where I'm calling

in a circle, I picked up my heart, my hopes, my dreams, myself, my all,
my calling, in a circle

circles, life moves, in circles
not as meaningless motion, but as continuous action
round or octagonal, they may be interrupted, but can never be broken
circles, faith grows, in circles
circles, grace flows, in circles
in circles, forever and ever amen, in circles

Rebirth

a picture is worth a thousand words
or maybe it's just one

and maybe the one word
changes like the seasons, the wind, the position of the sun

and maybe the one word
transforms into something new
evolves into something more complete

and maybe the one word
reimagines itself
like a spirit that's been shattered
a calling that's been shamed into silence

and maybe it's not the picture that holds a thousand words
but one word that frames the picture

and this day
two years later
after my face was plastered in the paper
maybe one word is more than enough

rebirth

{Pentecost}

Grace Is

grace is amazingly unexplainable and utterly illogical
yet seems to be the answer or the excuse for everything
and ordinands are asked to describe it in 300 words or less

grace is vulnerable and allows us to be vulnerable
grace is predictable and surprising
and helps us live with the unthinkable
and ushers in the impossible
and holds us when the unimaginable becomes real

grace is free but not cheap
it will cost you everything
including the ability to withhold it from others
if it's not for all it's not for you

you'll know you're in her presence
when us and them becomes we
when fears and judgments vanish and so does modesty
when the glass suddenly looks like it's just been wiped clean
and even though there is a cloud of grief above you
the horizon is clear

grace is a mirror reflecting our image back to us
not as we are but as god made us
and as we could be if we'd only…

grace is progressive and traditional
and like our life span has stages
like eternity it's always been
but there comes a time when we recognize it
and examine it
and try it on for size
and then we claim it like god claimed us
and then it begins to change us
and shape us
and when growing pains us grace sustains us
and in those fleeting moments of perfection grace celebrates with us

grace is a gift to us but she isn't ours
we are just one of a creation full of recipients

how amazingly foolish to think we are more deserving than another
that grace is earned or exclusive

grace flows like psalmic streams and ancient songs
from baptismal fonts and IV bags and rain from dented eaves troughs
and tears from sorrow-swollen eyes

grace rises
like freshly kneaded dough baked into nourishing loaves of bread
and cakes and cookies and tortillas and scones
like a community coming to the table for a meal and for a prayer
like a child walking to the microphone to sing a solo for the first time
like women marching
like black mothers standing up to speak their slain daughters' names
oh, Sandra and Breonna
like hope in the midst of soul piercing pain

grace fills our cups to the brim
and flavors our drinks like freshly squeezed lemon
and a long anticipated slice of orange

grace fills our hearts with comfort
when we come out of our closet only to be backed into a corner
grace sits with us
listens to all the reasons we have for wanting to quit
and gathers all the towels we want to throw in
and makes a quilt of them
and gives us one night of warmth and peaceful rest

and then in the morning grace fills us with the courage
to get up and to live again
with two fingers under our chin
she instructs us to hold our head high again
and like only grace can say
says,
don't let them destroy you
I know your name, beloved you are mine

water is life and grace is present
anywhere and everywhere water flows and even when it's stagnant
or comes to us only in medically designed drips through tubes carefully
inserted into our veins

bread is life and grace is present
anytime and every time bread and people rise to eat or to be heard

the cup is life and grace is present in it
in every flavor
both sweet and bitter
natural or artificial

grace is amazingly unexplainable
grace is in our current denomination held hostage and unrecognizable
grace will not be mocked and unlike votes cannot be bought
grace isn't dying
but we are

god is grace and grace is present
even when and maybe more so when a presider is not
when prayers come from the heart and not the script

god is good and grace is too
even when humans are not

god is love and grace is too
even when the united methodist church is not

god cries and grace does too
when hearts and minds are closed
and doors are locked

god weeps and grace does too
when grace is the answer to why I am allowed in
and the excuse for keeping you out

grace is amazingly unexplainable
and utterly illogical

grace is
out of bed and up in her chair today
talking and drinking
and dreaming about her next meal
she really wants a bowl of grits

grace is a fighter
and so am I
grace and I are holding each other
tightly
so neither can quit

grace is…

Confirmation

today you will be baptized
I pray for you and for your family
the one made of blood and the one born of water and the spirit
I pray that in this moment god's voice is still enough for us to hear it

hush...do you hear it?

on this day, the dove descends just low enough for us to reach up and touch it
whispers just loud enough for us to hear it say
you, yes you are pleasing and good and exactly enough

and I pray for this water, stirred by love's own hand
not that it would be made sacred and holy because by nature it is and always has been

I pray that when this water is poured out upon you
you will know without a doubt what has always been true
that god has unconditional love for you
that you have worth beyond measure and value greater than any piece of gold or silver
that from the crown of your head to the souls of your feet you are perfect
exactly who god made you to be

I pray that as those drops of water roll down your face
your skin will absorb an eternal amount of grace
and that it will sink so far into your soul
that nothing will ever cause you to question its power
and that it will saturate your heart so completely
that should anyone ever dare to challenge your humanity you will not be shaken
but will find the strength to stand tall and proud and reject their lies

I pray for us who promise to nurture and support you
may we know how serious this is, that this moment, that this water
like an umbilical cord binds us together forever
that none of us can eat alone, or breathe alone, or survive alone

with this water on you we remember the water poured out on us
in this we mix the mortar of community

your baptism is when you claim the precious knowledge that god
claimed you
and may we vow to never let you forget this good news
in times of confidence or uncertainty
on a mountain or in a valley and all the places in between may we
journey with you

today you will be confirmed
I pray for you and for this commitment you make
and for the family you bring with you and for this family you enter into
I pray that in this moment Jesus' voice is clear enough for us to
comprehend it

careful…do you hear him?

on this day, our brother is close and speaking
reminding us, *the church is the people*

and today I pray for the people, particularly for you
and for the church, especially this one that houses me and you

you're joining a church that like the world is broken
maybe what it needs to be whole is you
maybe what's been missing is you
your gifts, your presence
your talents, your service, your dreams, your visions

we know what Jesus said about the stone that the builders rejected
I pray that you may never know rejection and I pray that you will rise
in dissent
should this church ever again reject any one of god's children
and god forbid you do experience the pain of rejection
woe to us who do not risk it all to fight for you

I pray that your hands will model love and your feet walk in peace
and your voice speak life and your eyes focus on justice

and your heart attune to mercy, and your ears hear where the spirit is calling and that your center will always be the cornerstone

I pray for us
may our example always be worthy of emulation
slow to anger, hesitant to judge
quick to forgive, willing to resist, and free from hypocrisy

so, your baptism, your glorious welcome into the family of faith
I pray that it fills you and continues to feed you
and that you will feed those starving around you

and your confirmation, your relationship with this church, with the church universal
I pray that it will build you up and gird you up
and that by your witness a denomination sinking from leaks and cracks
will be shored up and sealed and secured and become again a firm foundation
safe for all creation for all the ages
and may it—no—if like grace we claim it
it will be so

Letters to St. Louis

all this talk about St. Louis
and part of me wants to run for the hills
to another denomination
to a world that doesn't recognize organized religion
but for today the spirit is calling me to be still

those letters such betrayals, so much too little too late
that say so much yet say so little
that seek silence from the oppressed and sympathy for the oppressor
that belittle the pain of those who wrote their own letters
honest letters, agonizing letters
hopeful, without the help of a committee of editors, gospel filled letters
letters that got no response or a patronizing, dismissive reply

could you add a sentence explicitly stating that you're not practicing
god works in mysterious ways
is this because you wish to get married
if you're not in a relationship why rock the boat
are you in a relationship
you're not, are you
there are ways to remain closeted
it's only an issue if you make it one
surely the UCC would be glad to take you
if the rules change and I'm still a bishop I'll welcome you back
if the rules change and it gets worse I might not be able to stay myself
have you thought about staying in your position as a lay person
what about the people who are harmed by the lack of more punitive consequences to
violations of the book of discipline
this is hard for us too
on a scale of 1-10 just how happy are you
it's been more than three months, but the board of ordained ministry confirms
receipt of your letter and acknowledges that perhaps we are a group of cowards

I sometimes wish I were a literalist
that whole thing about god spewing out the lukewarm
a reference to the centrist wanting to unite us
proclaiming the power to save us, advocating the middle of the road as
the safest

so yes
all these letters scripting the road to St. Louis are writing havoc in my head
I lay in bed at night reciting the alphabet forwards and backwards hoping to fall asleep
replaying words and conversations, wishing I could rearrange and re-write them
but as hard as these years have been I don't regret sending them
yes, they seemingly cost me everything, but they also lead me to my freedom
because now those letters I can claim them, name them
openly be them, celebrate my part in them
LGBTQIA

I'm not fighting them, hiding them, denying them
trying to erase them from my soul by burning them from my skin
I'm not running from them and today with the spirit's hand upon me
I'm not running from anything or to anything
I'm being still
I'm listening
I'm living in the moment
I'm playing with letters at night when I can't sleep
instead of desperately crying or planning an escape
while my mind is trying to flee to St. Louis my feet are right here
and my hands and my heart are grounded in something unexplainably real

this morning as I watched a young boy rearrange foam letters
on the church nursery room floor
proudly spelling big words and little words and making new shapes out of them
I was reminded that letters
written on paper with institutional ink aren't where my faith is found
and those three years with those three letters in front of my name
didn't spell the real me
and surrendering them didn't erase my place among the called

all this talk about St. Louis
and part of me wants to run for the hills and maybe one day I will
but that day is not today

if you're looking for me
you will find me with the foam, rainbow colored letters being still
still being the one the united methodist church baptized, confirmed,
and commissioned
sitting, serving alongside others
designing new ways, reimagining old words
using all the letters
all the letters of the alphabet and ones that haven't been singled out yet
writing our way forward
building our path
not to St. Louis, but to the holy
to kin-dom
to community
together

{Extraordinary}

Unraveling

in my pocket there's a piece of fabric
all rolled up with a little lipstick on it
here's how it all unraveled

I never sought out a robe
an alb as the saleswoman at the church supply store called it
never quite felt comfortable in it
even with a nice belt, a cincture as my clergy mentor described it
I don't like to stand out or be noticed

and walking down an aisle to music
praying, preaching, standing in front of a crowd teaching
in a big cream colored alb made me feel very noticed
made me believe my doubt and shame was obvious
all I ever wanted—was called to do—was pray and preach and teach
and show others that if god could use one like me
then surely god could use them too

and not use, like one does an old piece of fabric to wipe up a spill
or patch a quilt
but use, like an artist paints a picture of a single flower
growing in a snow-covered field to depict hope
or like the beloved church mother kissing your cheek
leaving a little lipstick behind to deliver the gospel truth

for some three years I went through the motions of putting on the alb
fighting the voice of doubt it projected
trying to silence the song that rang from its many creases and wrinkles
that no amount of ironing or pleading could remove
and my praying and preaching and teaching started to wane
my life, every shadowy, bruised, blood stained moment became caught
up in the fabric of the alb and I couldn't shake it

I knew that if I was ever going to heal, love and accept myself, quit
feeling like a fraud, I had to do something with that alb, all that itchy
fabric

and I certainly couldn't continue in the process
and let some bishop put a stole over top of it
that would make it way too heavy to ever get it off of me again

ordination would be the nail in the coffin, or truer yet for me, the dead
bolt on the closet
the last time I wore it was when I stood shaking in a pulpit
sharing out loud what I didn't think I'd ever say
not again, it hadn't gone so good the first time
and I said it, what I couldn't keep silent about for another day
I told the church I'm lesbian and not going to hide it
and am not here to offer up my life for denominational politics
because I am not called to that
there are those that are
let's celebrate that and respect that there are those that are not
and hold in tension the emotions involved in that
many and great o god are the emotions

but back to the fabric at hand or rather in my pocket
all rolled up with a little lipstick on it
out of the closet, down from the pulpit
the beloved 90 year old church mother called me over
motioned me to sit beside her and she said,

I tried so hard, but couldn't hear your message, will tell me what you
said
I gave the cliff note version
harder to deliver than the original
with tears in her eyes she clenched her hand into a fist
shook it in the air and with what little voice she could muster
whispered
oh, this church has done it again
then she pulled me in kissed my face and said
I love you

no judgment, no litany of questions, no personal commentary or reflections
just love and a place to rest my head
one of the kisses missed my cheek and landed on the alb
or the robe as most ordinary people call it

when I decided to get rid of it
I left it out in the rain for days wanting to wash a little bit of the joy
and pain away
and then I deconstructed it one thread at time, except one little piece
and then I walked the remnants to the dumpster
like walking down the center aisle to receive new bread and new wine
in my pocket there's a piece of fabric
all rolled up with a little lipstick on it
a reminder of a love that cannot be unraveled

Tables, Leaves, and Forks

my grandparents always had a beautiful dining room table with several
leaves
set perfectly for holidays, special occasions, and Sunday meals
each setting set just right
plates, salad plates, and crystal water glasses

my young unsophisticated self completely confused
and mesmerized by the position of the silverware
there's too many forks
I prayed that someday I'd know which fork to use for what
and the cloth napkins, oh, the cloth napkins with brass holders
that matched the table cloth, the runner, the candles in the middle
made me feel royal
my life more like a cheap paper napkin cried out silently for something
to hold me together

that magically, majestically set table capturing my attention
stirring me to strive for something better
like the wooden spoon stirring the dumplings in the pot
slicing away the pain, carving out a will to survive
like the freshly sharpened knife gliding through the prime rib
was merely a dream, a fantasy, a fairytale
so far from my reality

there was a card table in the other room with metal folding chairs
reserved for the young ones, the in-laws and outlaws
the plates were different
a step above paper, certainly not china
the silverware less in number and value
only one fork
the paper napkins, of course, had no holders
the meat, dumplings and potatoes sitting on a dull plain dish not a
family heirloom platter
no candles, no runners, a simple plain cloth covering the torn leather
top of the wobbly table

I haven't subjected myself to those family meals in years
and I found another family that treated me the same
that let me close to the big table but only as a servant or an observer
that created a second table for those it deems too young, too
unsophisticated, too uneducated, too poor, too black, too brown, too
queer, too...

it took me a long time
I'm ashamed, angry, and sad it took such a long time to recognize the
parallels between the tables
side by side they are remarkably, painfully, sinfully similar
I'm also malnourished, I've starved to death at both of them
a spiritual food desert
I gave away nutrients and sustenance I needed
making place and space and hearty dinners for others
thinking crumbs were enough to sustain me
believing I could serve my way to wholeness and health
hoping if I waited long enough I could let my candle shine without fear
of being snuffed out

in stepping back from the tables
eating a simple meal of my own choosing with company that makes
me smile
that in this happy hour a continent away from home seems like a feast
with the same care and attention I so readily garnished on others

I see so clearly, I hear so vividly
I touch so intimately, I smell so intensely
I taste so richly, I feel so deeply

all the years of wasting
of un-ordained and unnecessary fasting
seeking acceptance, approval, and affirmation

all the weight lost and gained
feeding, nibbling on leftovers, scraps, and second bests

all the possibilities
fresh ingredients and new recipes

all the signs pointing me away from these tables

the metal chair legs shrieking across the tile floor that once sounded
like an unused salad fork scraping down a chalk board menu
suddenly sound like traveling music
like magic
majestically holding me together like the brass holder of the napkin
I was never allowed to unfold

the spirit is cooking and baking while I know not where she's leading
or what goodness she is making
I trust with all my senses that in these days
of waiting and resting
praying and feasting
laughing and loving
she's setting a place for me
at a table with endless leaves and forks

On Tax collectors and Calling

after a relatively short wait in line I approached the counter
and told the representative that I was there to get a Florida driver's
license
after going over my papers and verifying my identity she said
you must agree to surrender your Michigan license
I nodded in agreement and she reached into a drawer
pulled out a pair of scissors and cut my old license in half
handing me one of the pieces back, *here you go, have a seat until your
number is called*

I stumbled to the closest chair
out of breath and with a sharp pain in my chest
like I'd been stabbed
I touched my forearm to see if I was bleeding
suddenly I was back in Michigan
the Florida tax collector's office transformed into the bishop's
the people around me now colleagues, supervisors, mentors, friends
no longer strangers and new neighbors with renewal notices and titles
to file

I imagine what I felt that day is what it would feel like to lead your own
funeral
to pick the songs and the prayers, to welcome the guests
to eulogize yourself, to spill your heart out
to speak your truth, to name your deepest sorrows and dreams
only to walk away empty
more than two years later there was still a veil of fog
keeping me from fully reliving or remembering that day
a protective layer of cognitive dissonance
in that most unlikely moment when an unknown participant quickly
tore it away

did everyone in that hot crowded room feel my pain and see my shame
were they looking at me with disgust
no, they were looking at the clock and their phones
and waiting anxiously for their numbers to be called
and photographs to be taken and applications to be accepted and
approved

there was no website or help line to call
no pamphlet on the wooden rack in the hall explaining the steps for
coming out
or how to do so while serving in a denomination where the rule book
simultaneously says you're a beautiful child of god and an abomination
where it was technically okay to be gay as long as you're not practicing
there was no workshop or plenary on how to have honest
conversations with people terrified of accidently saying something that
might be construed as queer affirming

I tried for months to figure out the right way
the procedurally appropriate way to say what I needed to say
every try another dead end or a question about my sexual practices or
relationship status
or an invitation into a deeper, darker closet
three years at the most, that's not that long to wait

I know there are those who still question my decision
who judge my leaving the way I did
just like this old man next to me still yelling because he can't sell a car
without a title
I want to stand up and scream, *that's the way it is*
and that's what I wanted to say to them
this whole situation is completely wrong, no one should ever be in this position
yet that's the way it is

I chose to surrender my credentials not because my calling ended or
my gifts dissipated
but because the cost of holding them was way too high
because to hold that title and hold my job I also held a lie
the weight of which was crushing me
and preventing me from holding the one thing that had gotten me this
far
grace—god's unending, unchanging, unconditional—grace
I handed the bishop my credentials
printed on paper that sat unopened in an envelope for years
creating space in my hands and my heart for grace
entering a place where I could open my eyes to grace
the ability to stand before a mirror and see the beauty of my own face

like those papers I kept myself concealed and hidden
afraid to be seen in the light

I surrendered my credentials not in defeat or hopeless submission
but in the hope of resurrection
that the me I had buried and burned and had beaten with self
damnation would rise
and live and find the joy she been taught to believe was undeserved

221, number 221 you're next
I got up to move to window 6
the sharp pain was gone, my breathing back to normal
the half of a driver's license in my hand seemed quite comical
the representative now helping me said
yeah, I don't know why we need to do that
what do they think you're gonna do with half a license

we both laughed, she asked me more questions
took my payment and then instructed me to go stand on the X behind
the blue line
smile
I smiled and 5 minutes later I had a new Florida driver's license
the photograph not so bad, much better than the one they cut still
resting in hand

a whole person, a complete, authentic person, number 221

February 21, 2017, the day I surrendered my credentials to make room
for my calling
the day I said yes to the holy and to the spirit calling
yes, I will follow where you're calling
I've spent years questioning that calling
believing that leaving left me without a future and a calling
doubting my worthiness and my calling
unable to realize that being me is part of the calling
it took a trip to the tax collector's office to finally see where all that
pain was leading
to freedom and to healing
which today are mine and are the substance of my calling

Conclusion and Call to Action

After penning these poems and unraveling throughout the liturgical year, I am now in a season of possibility and imagination. Pulling the threads on the hem of that robe led me to a new understanding of vocation and ministry. During that dry and lonely season of unraveling, I found healing balm, self-acceptance, and renewed purpose in the story of Rebekah, as shared in Genesis. Reading how she offered water to not only a traveler, but also to their ten camels, I re-discovered what I feared I lost. Released from the weight of vestments that never fit, I am free to live out a calling to authenticity and creativity.

The UMC unraveled me and writing poetry and creating 10 Camels bound me back together. Queer, quenched, whole, and affirmed I turn words into water through preaching, workshop facilitation, live poetry shows, and writing personalized worship resources, commissioned blessings, prayers, and poems nourishing individuals, churches, faith communities, and organizations who are thirsty for hope and healing.

God is with us in the unraveling, a guide as we pull the loose threads, a companion as we bound ourselves back together, a source of living water every step along the way.

Printed in the USA
CPSIA information can be obtained
at www.ICGtesting.com
LVHW010042210724
785816LV00004B/11

9 781960 326706